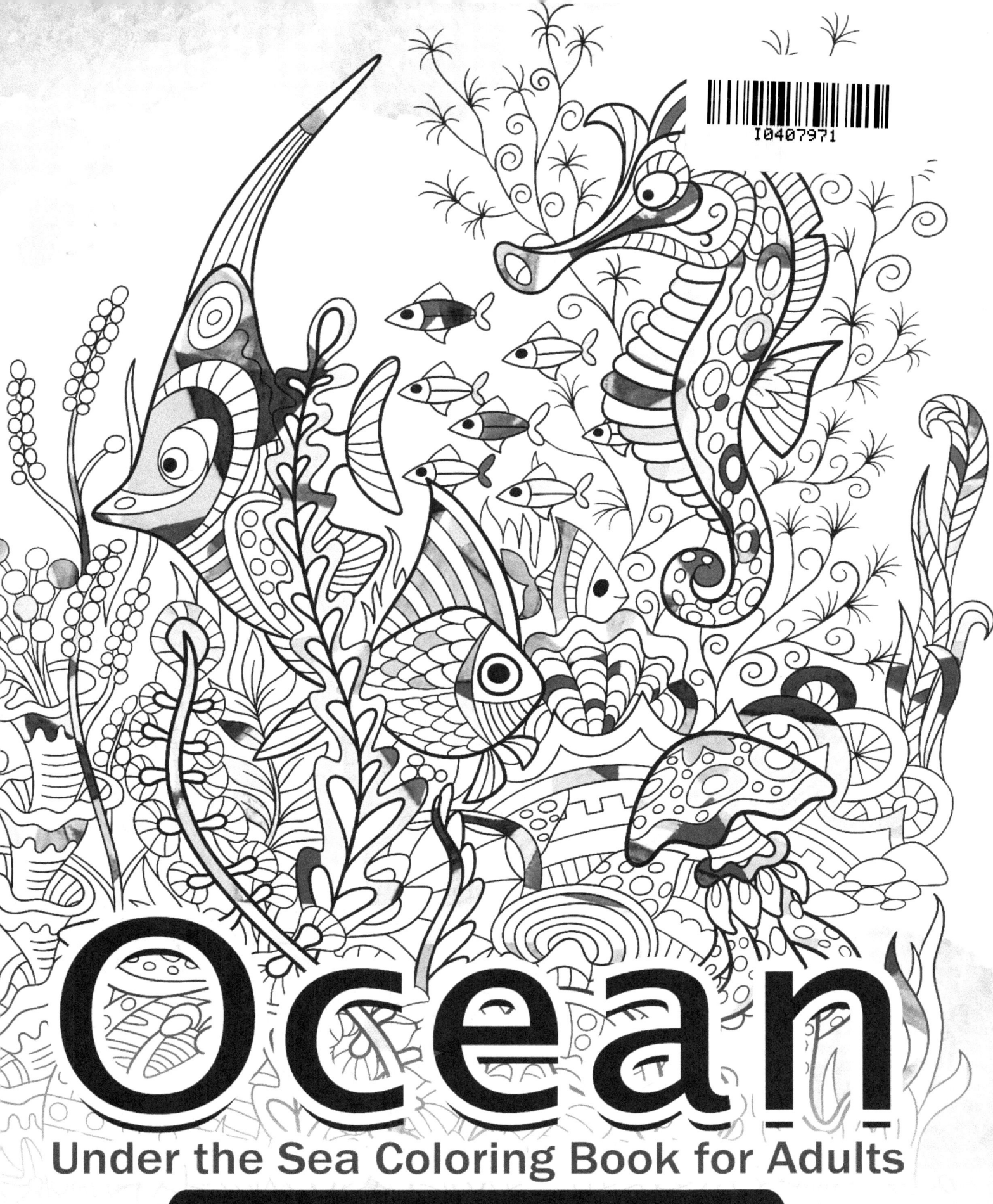

# Ocean

## Under the Sea Coloring Book for Adults

*Designs for Relaxation and Mindfuness*

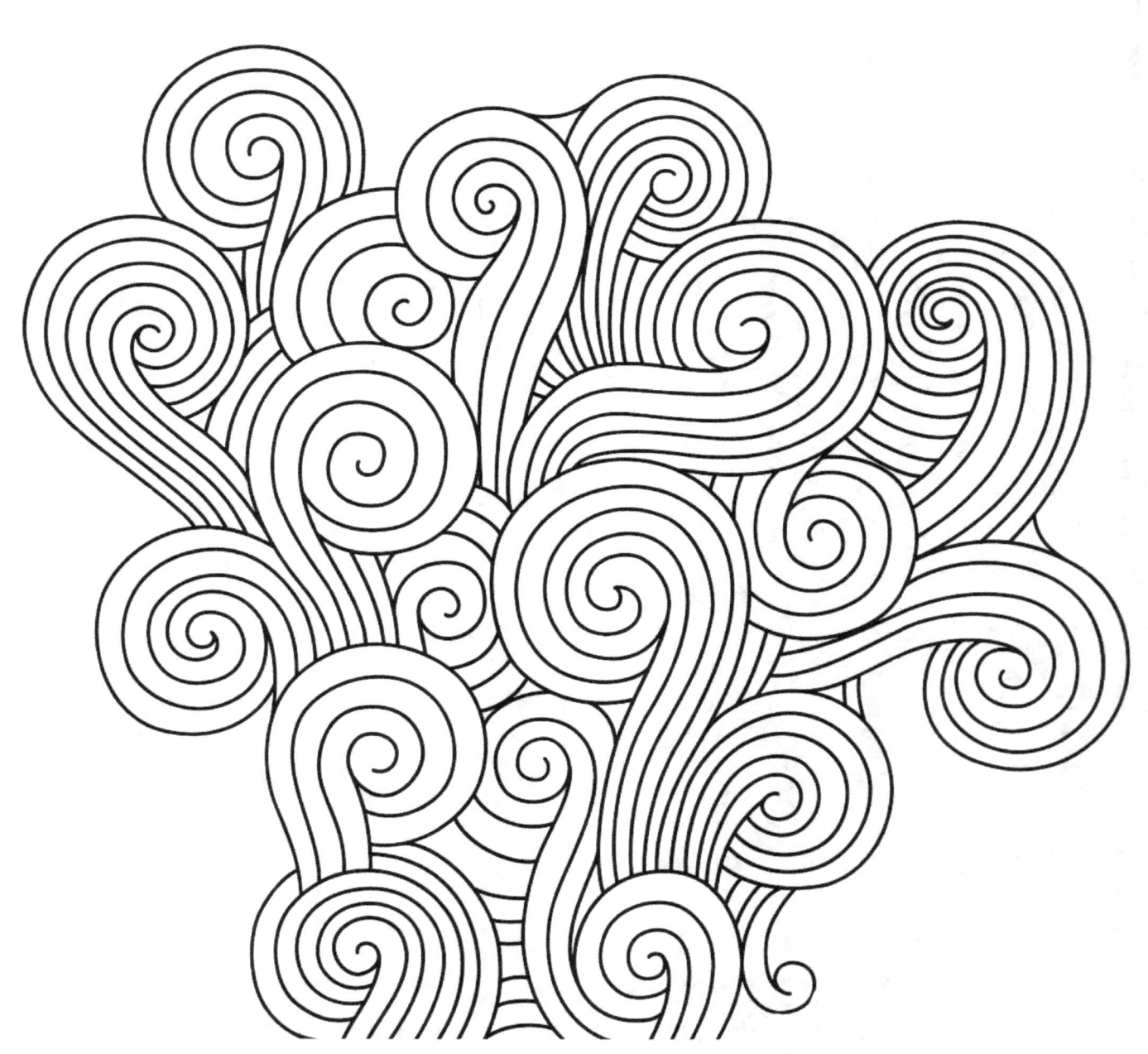

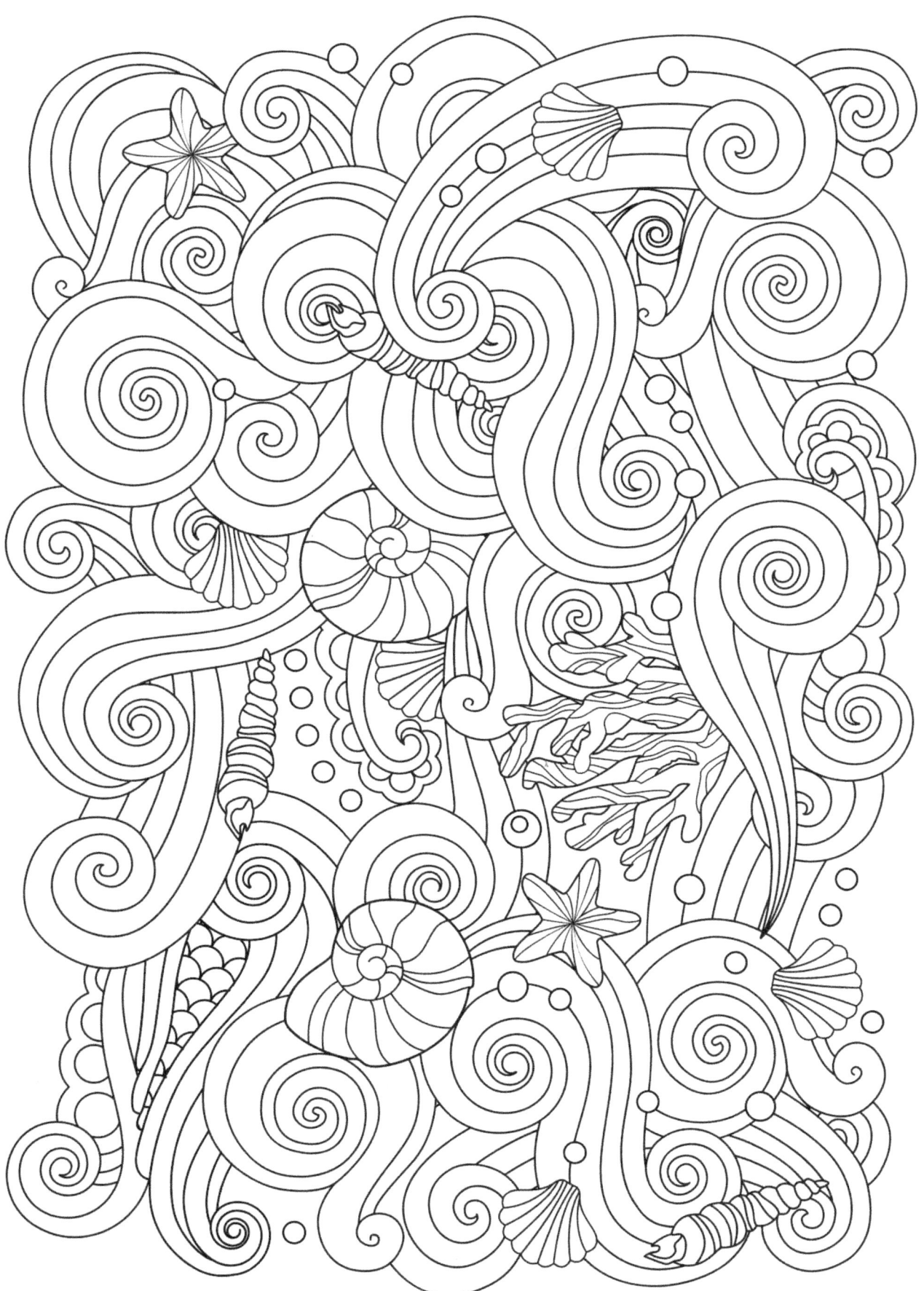

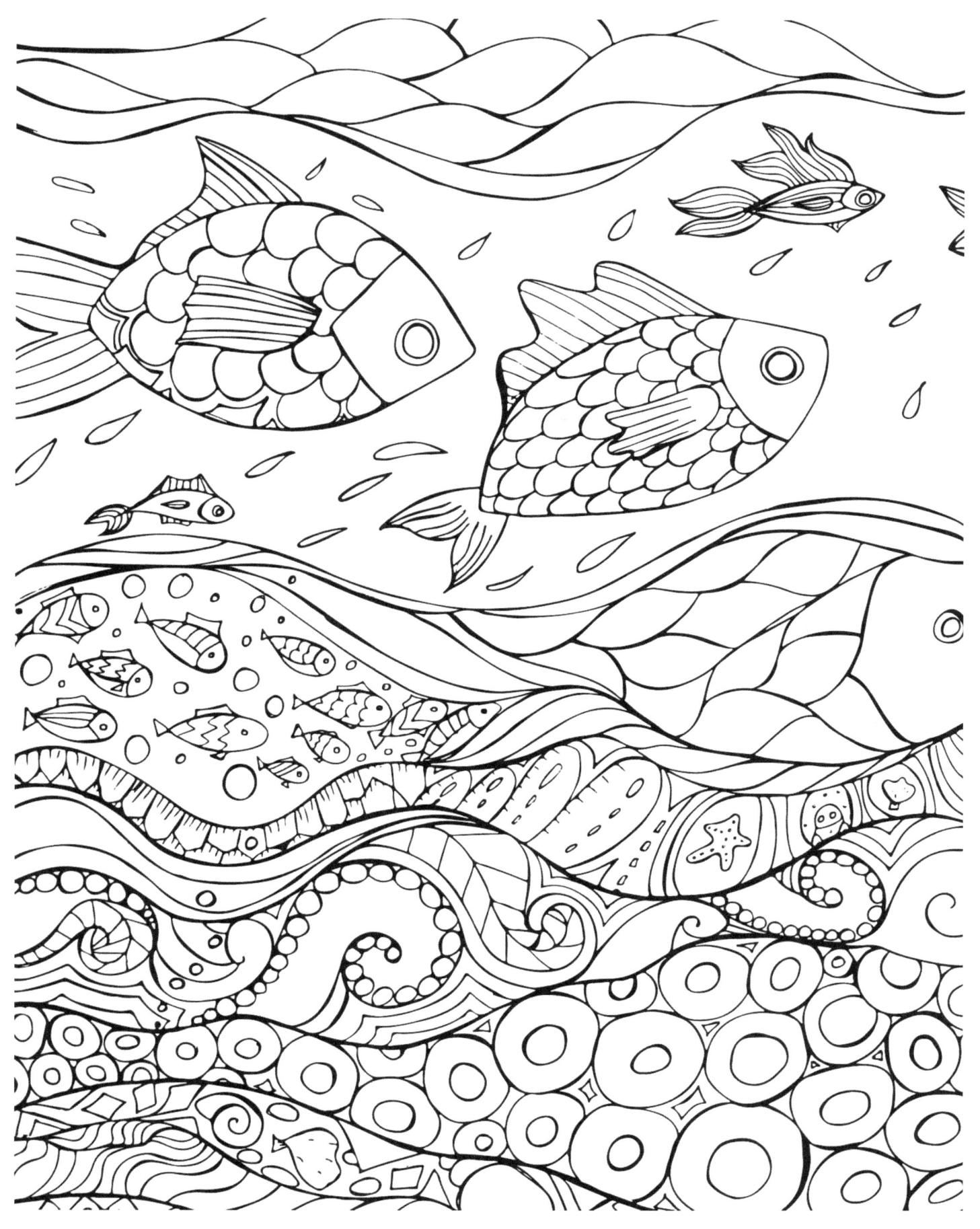

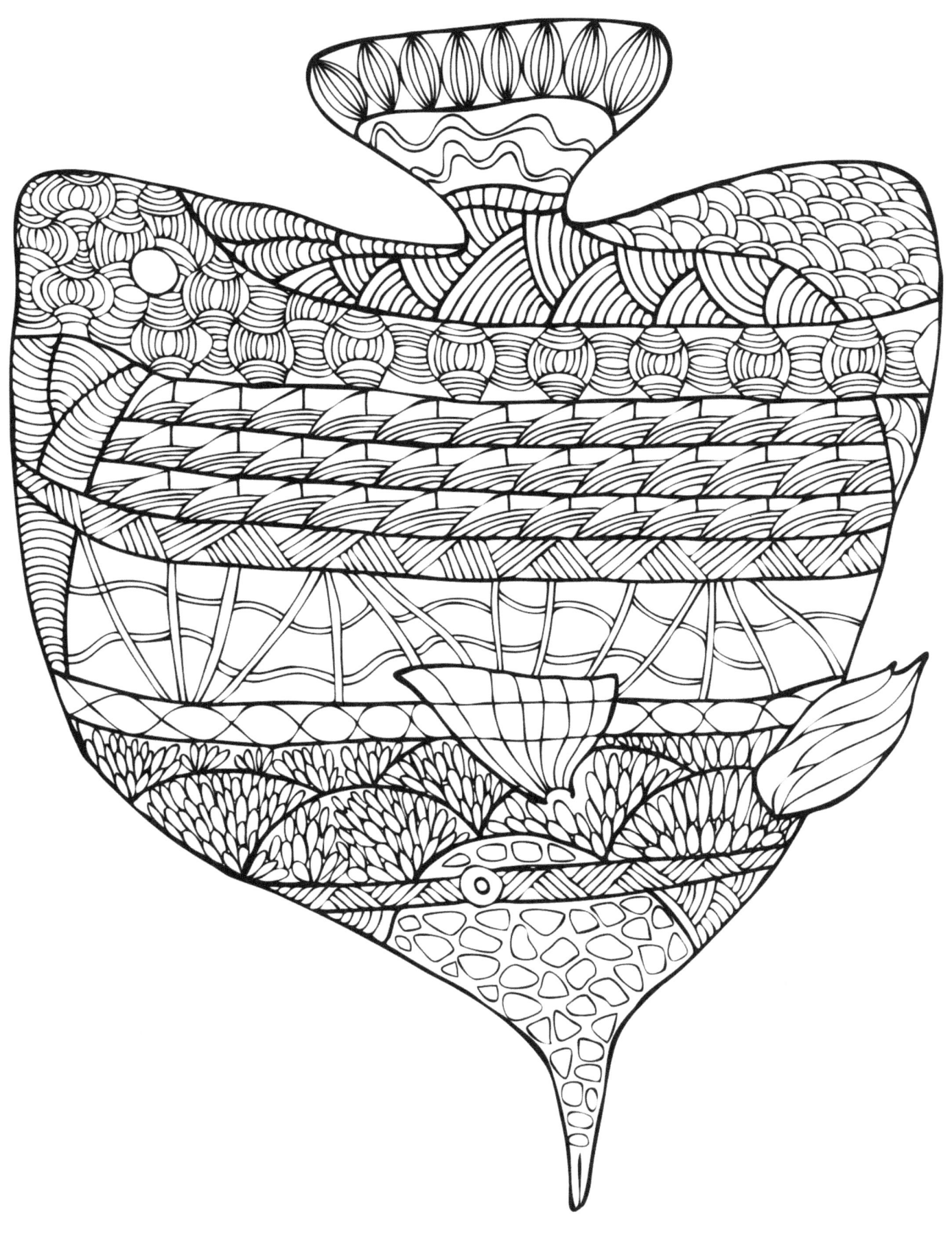

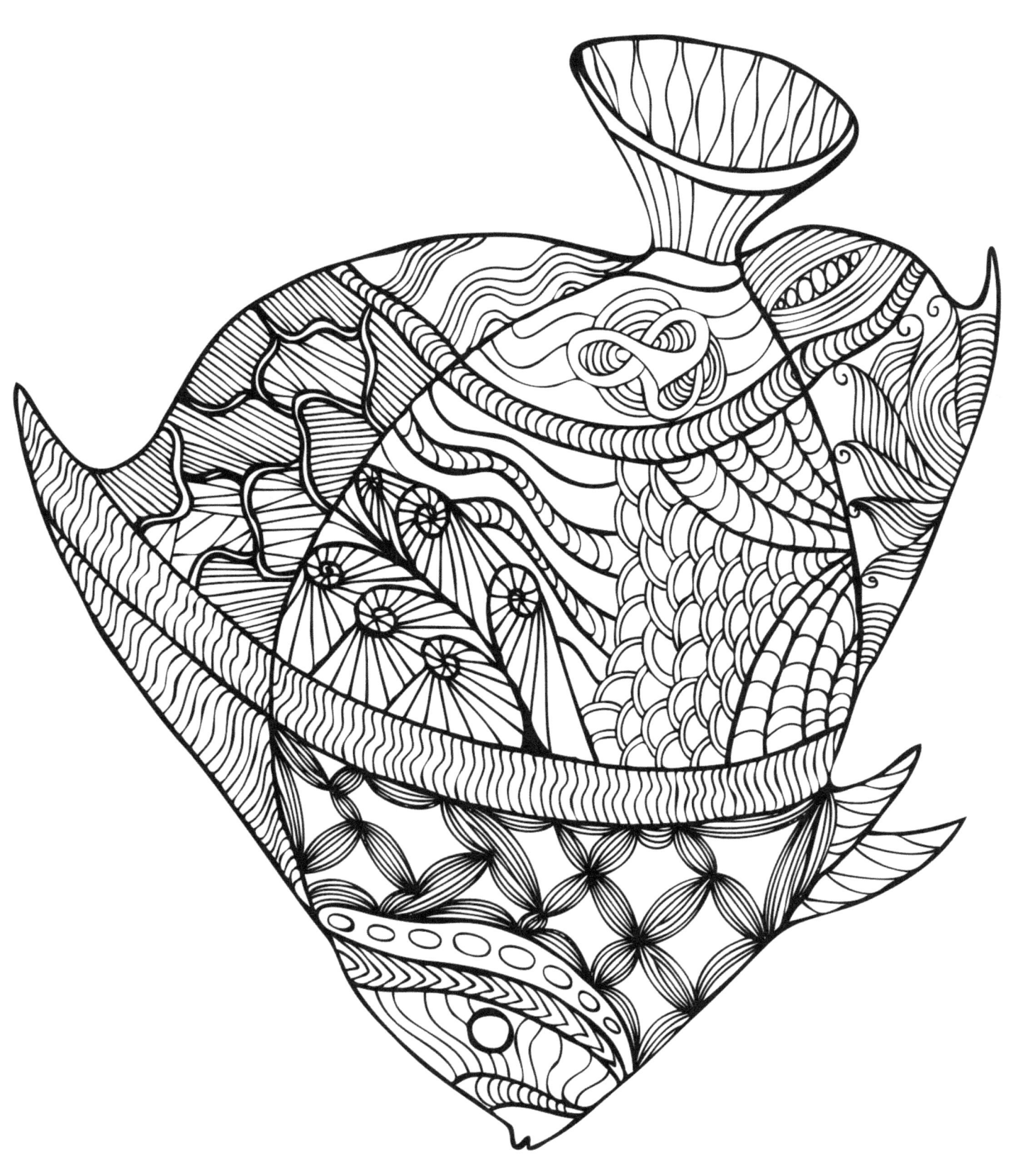

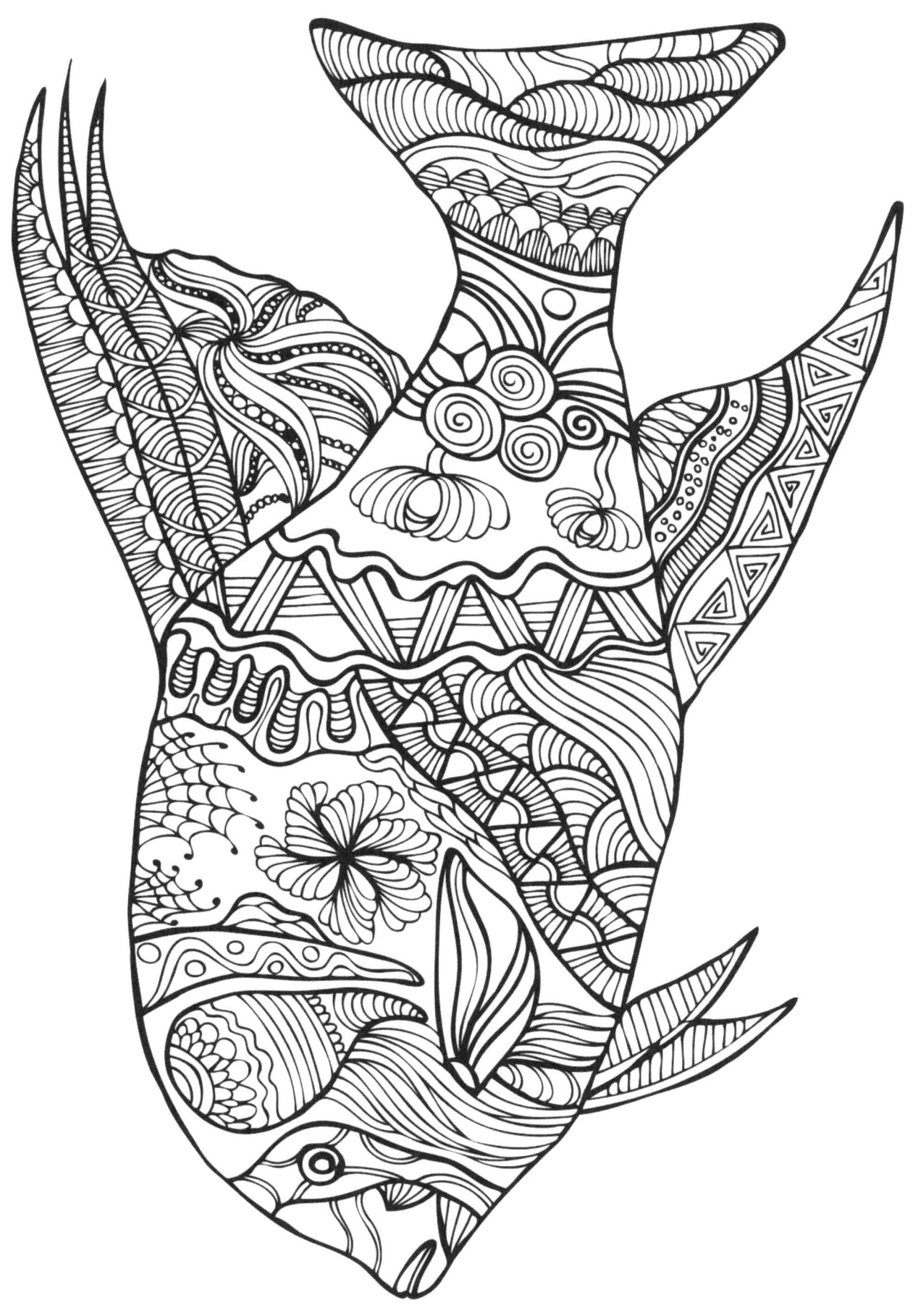

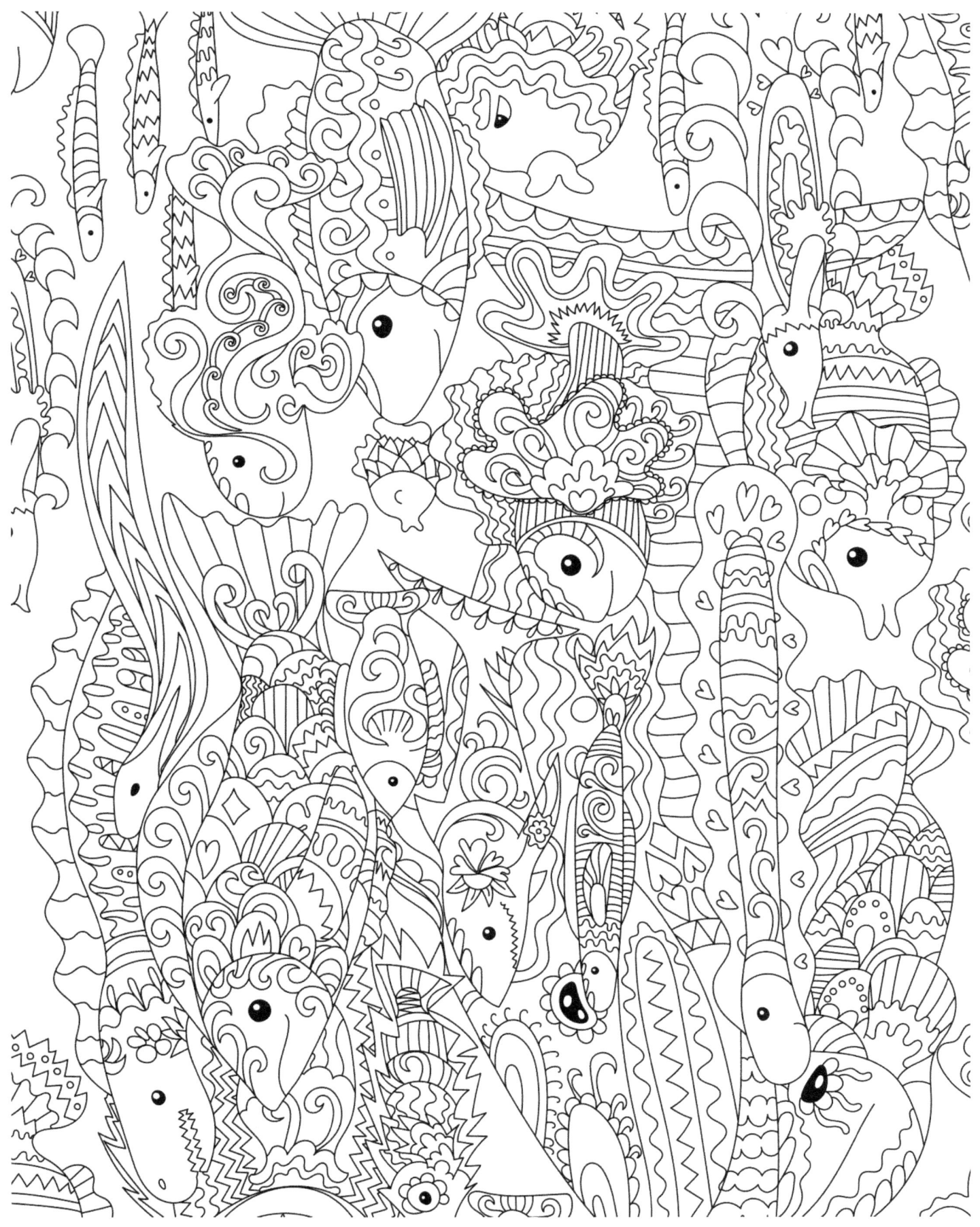

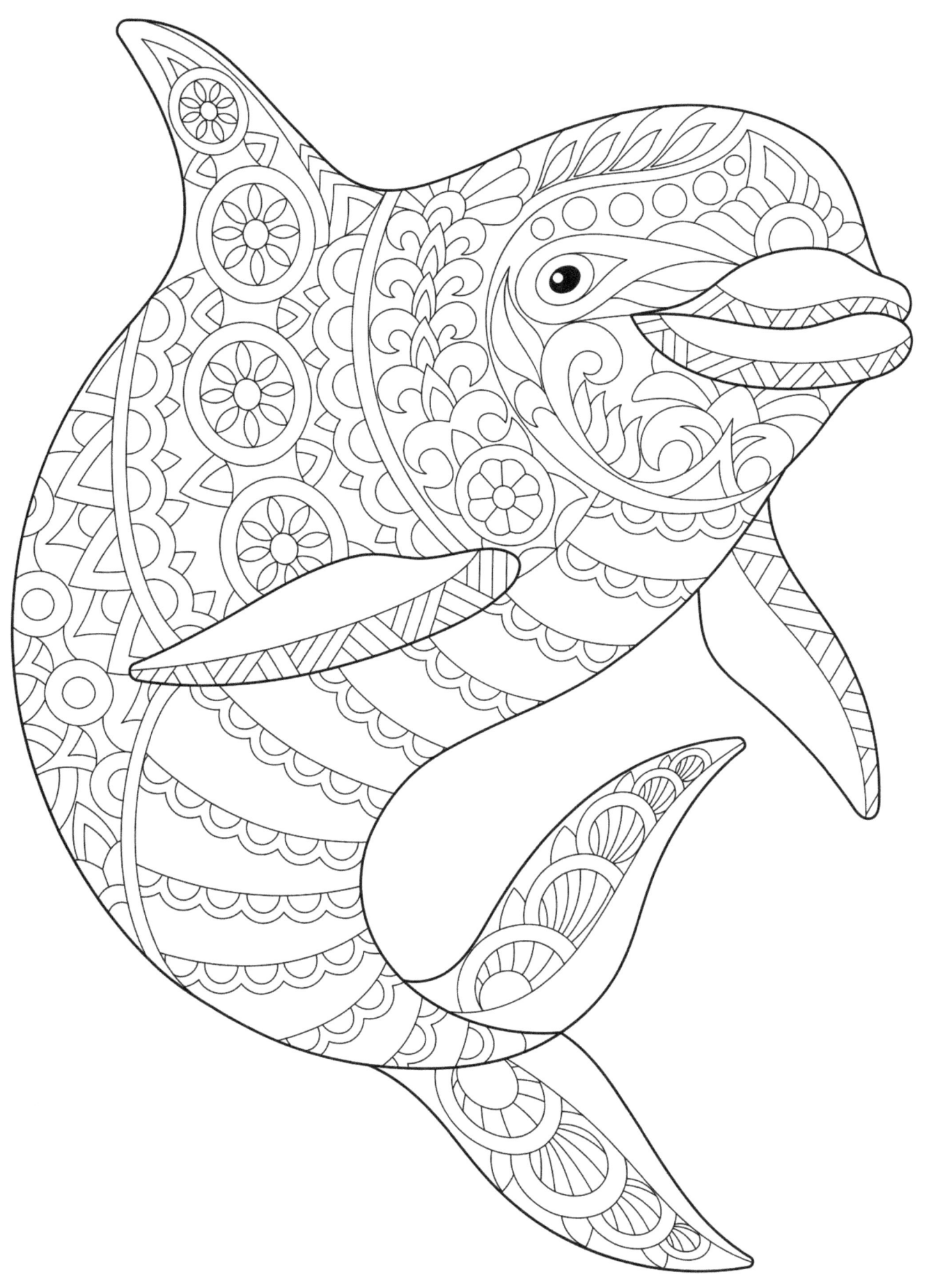

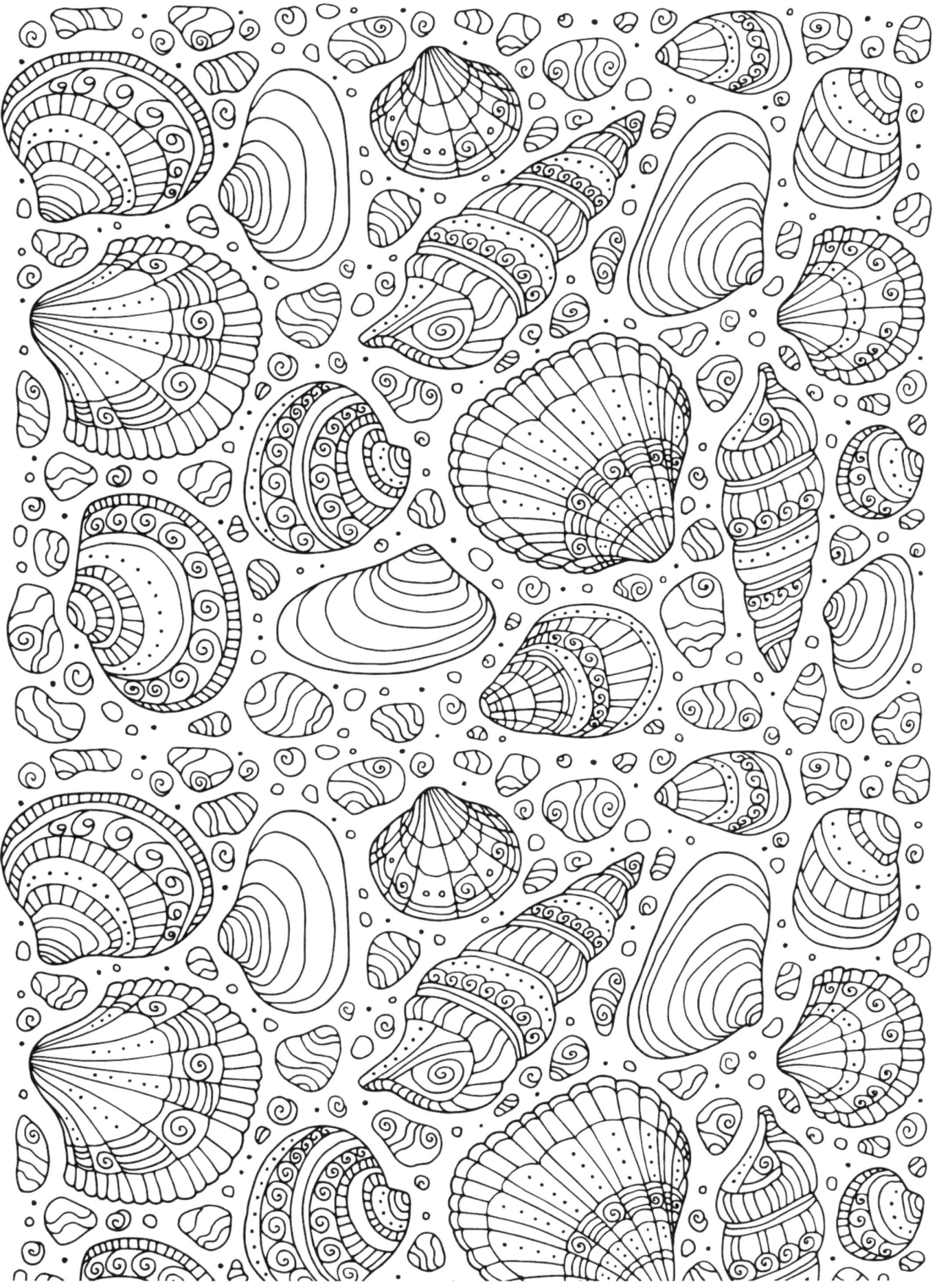

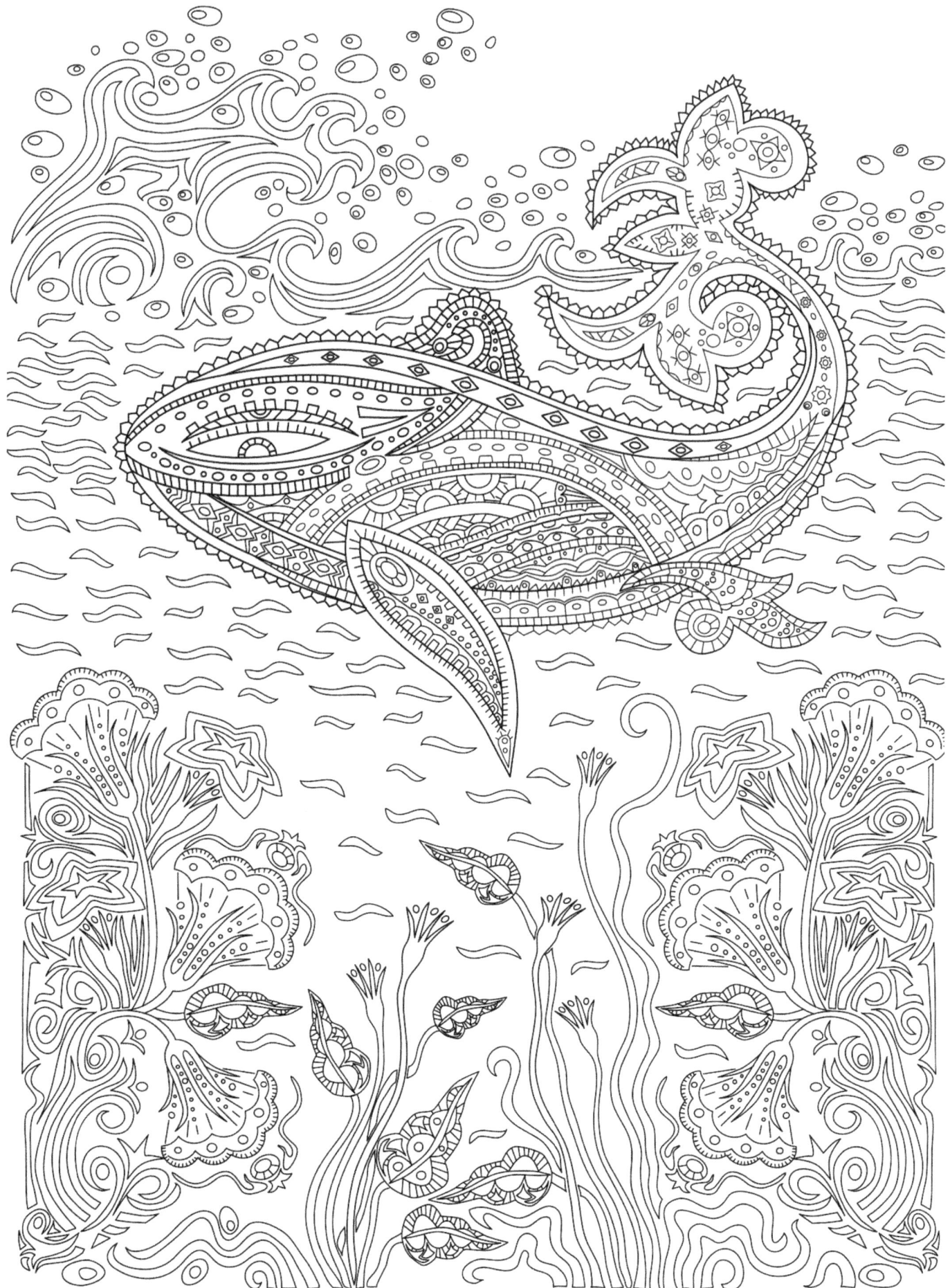

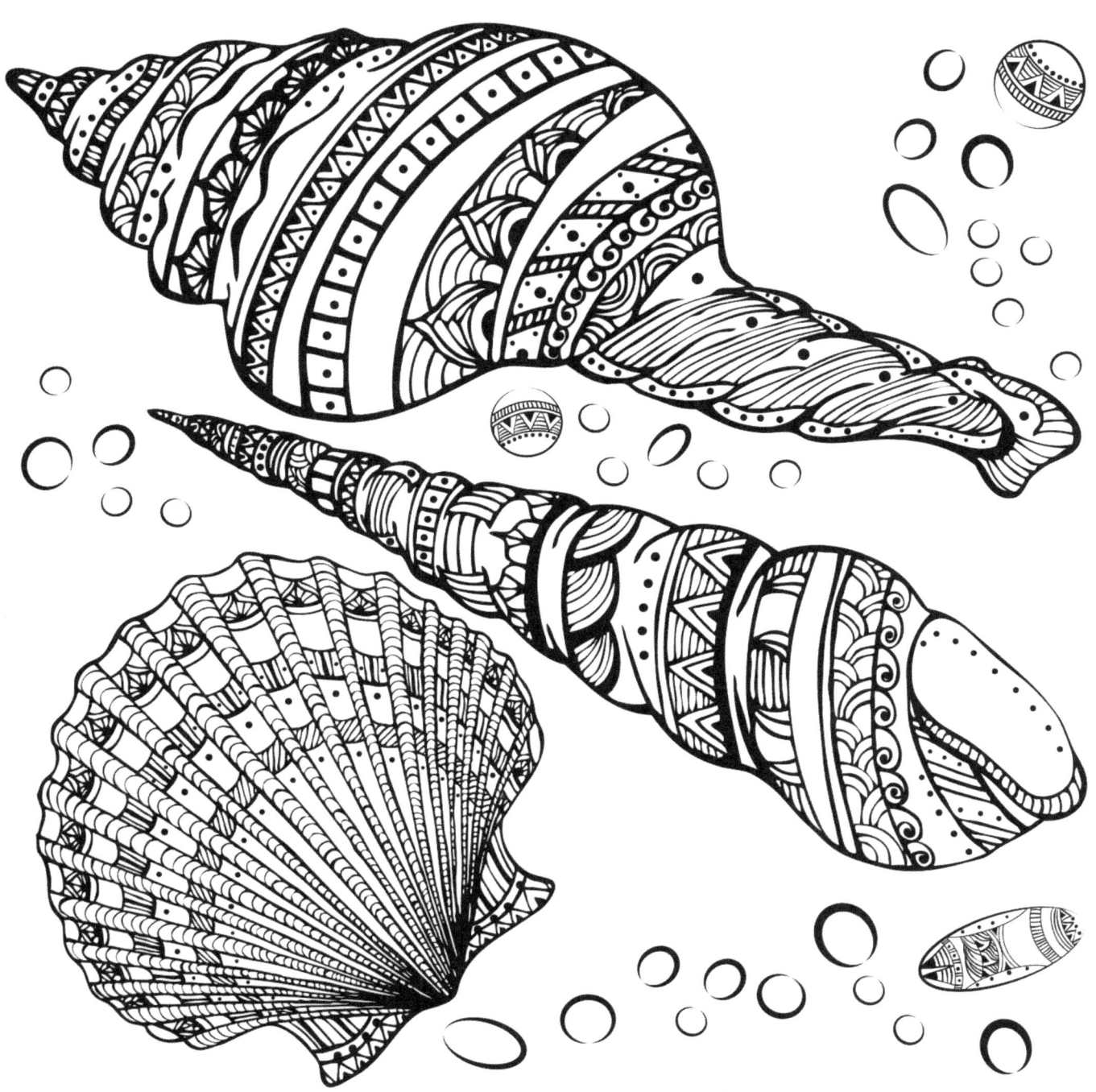

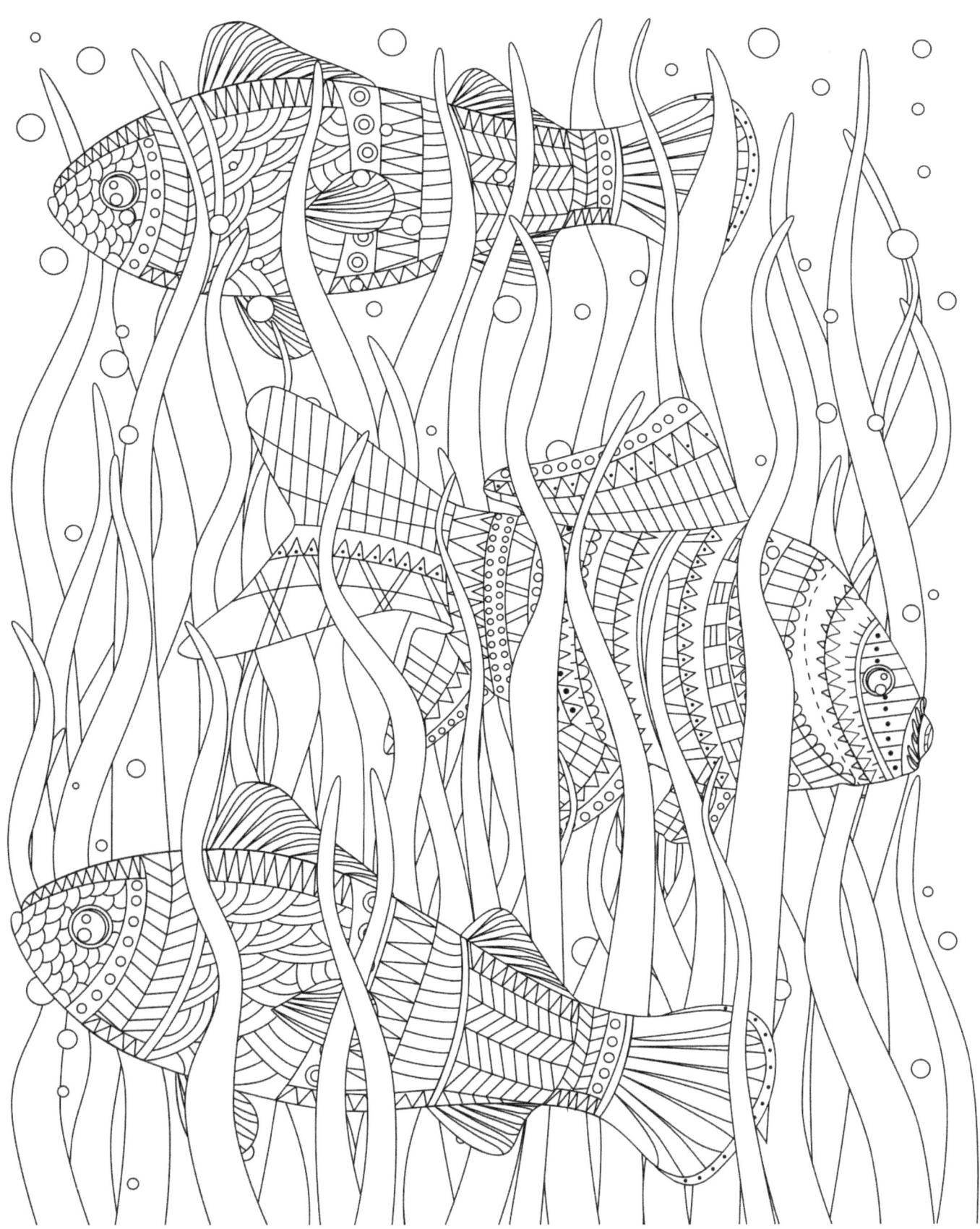

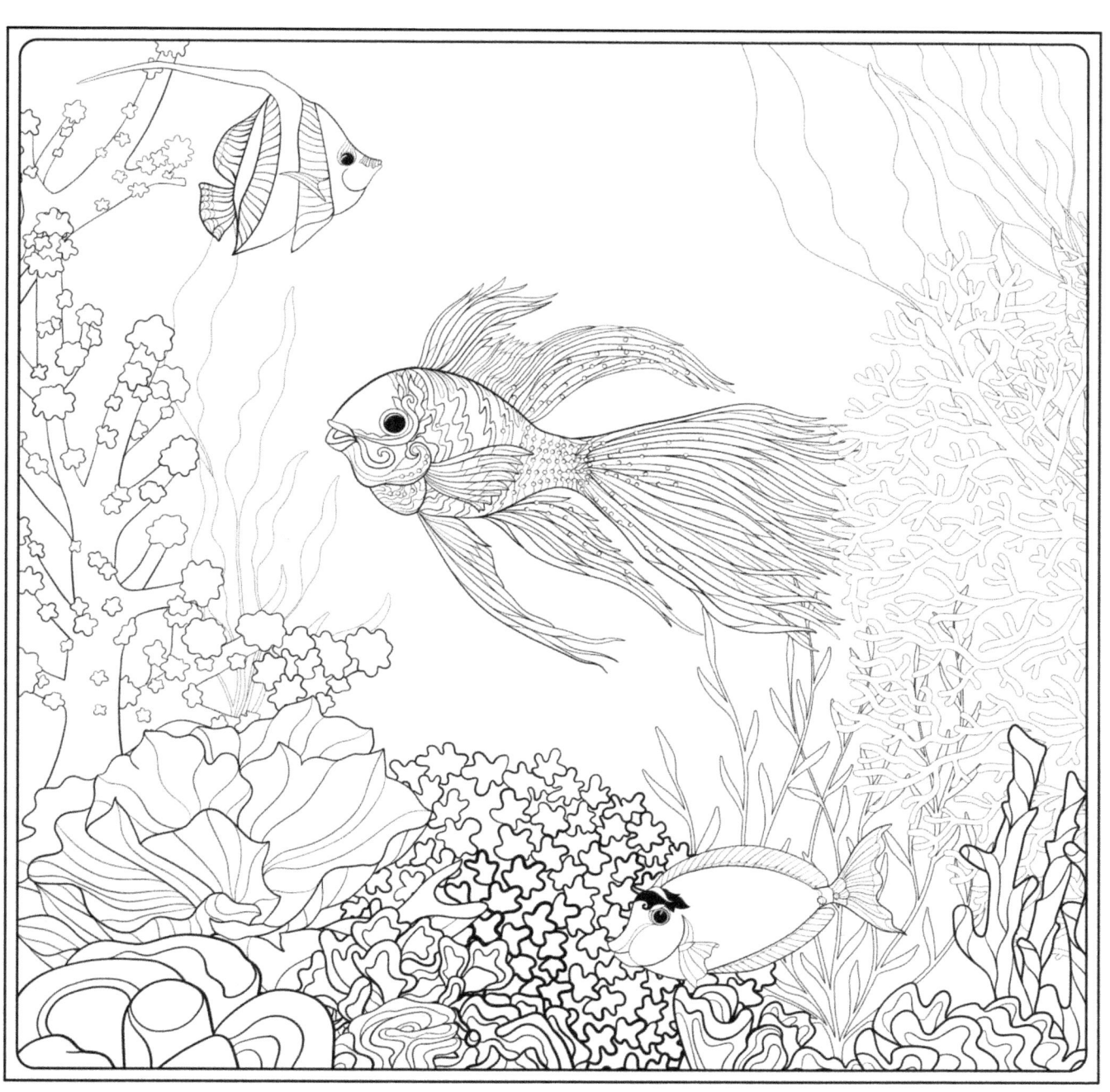

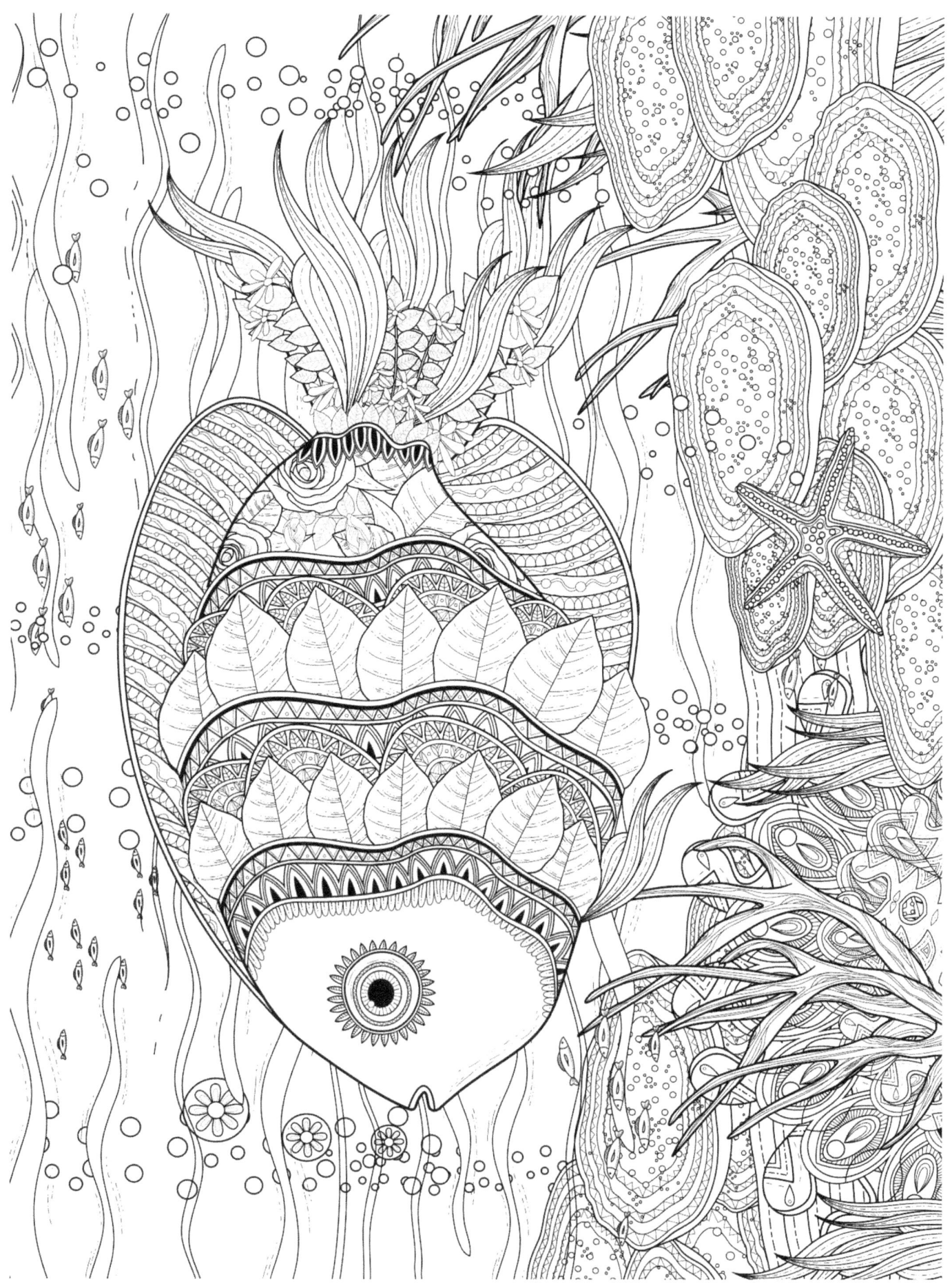

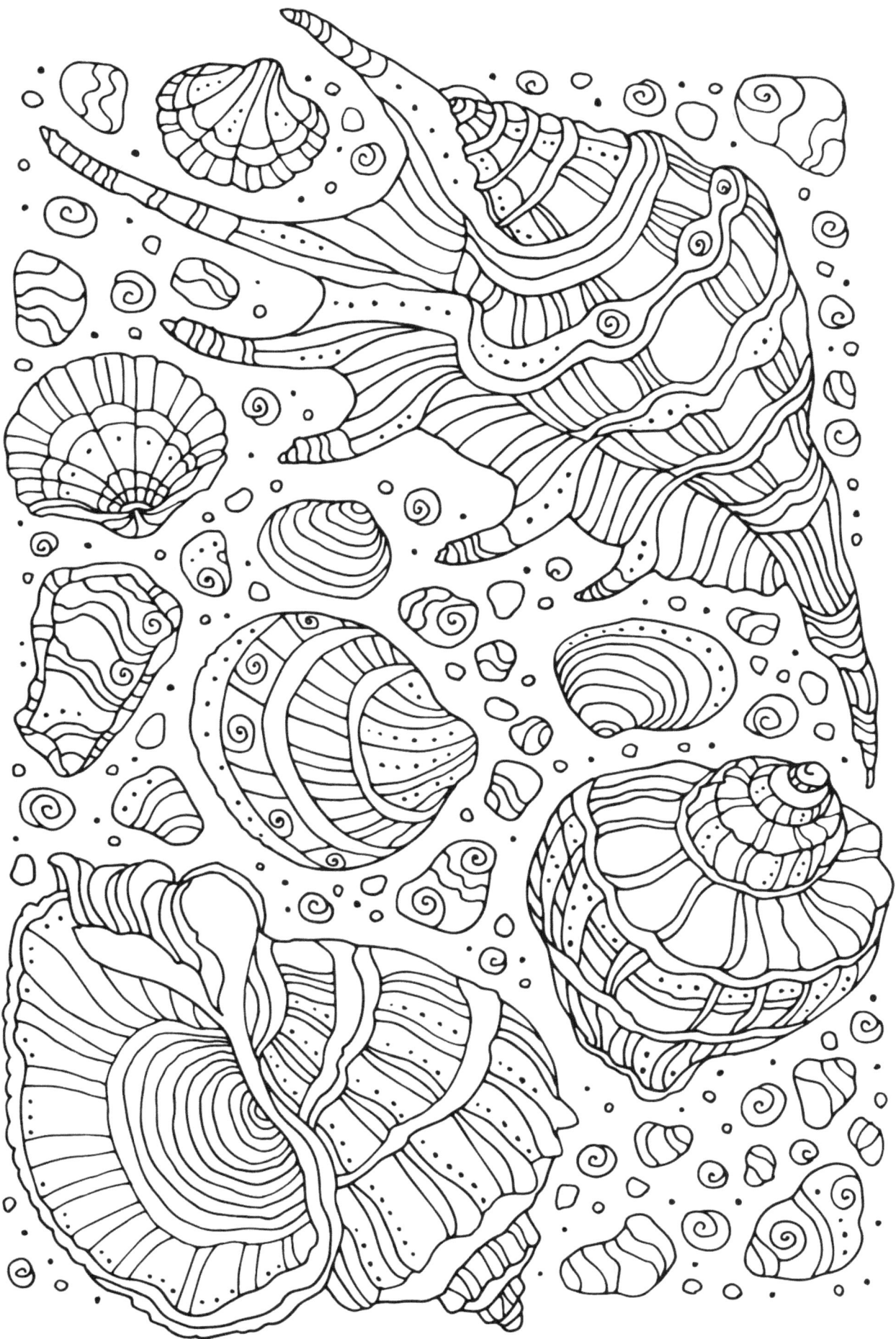

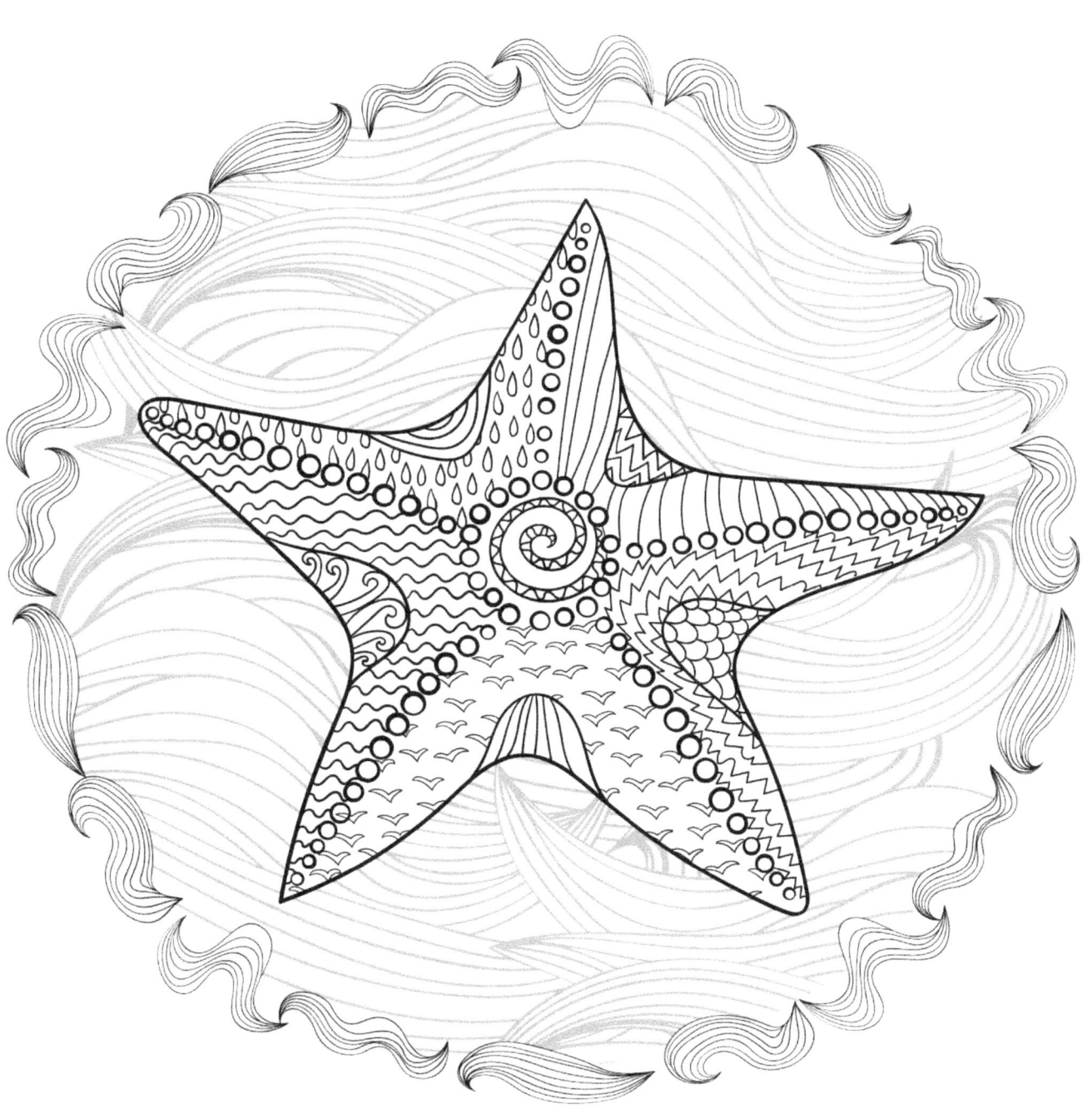

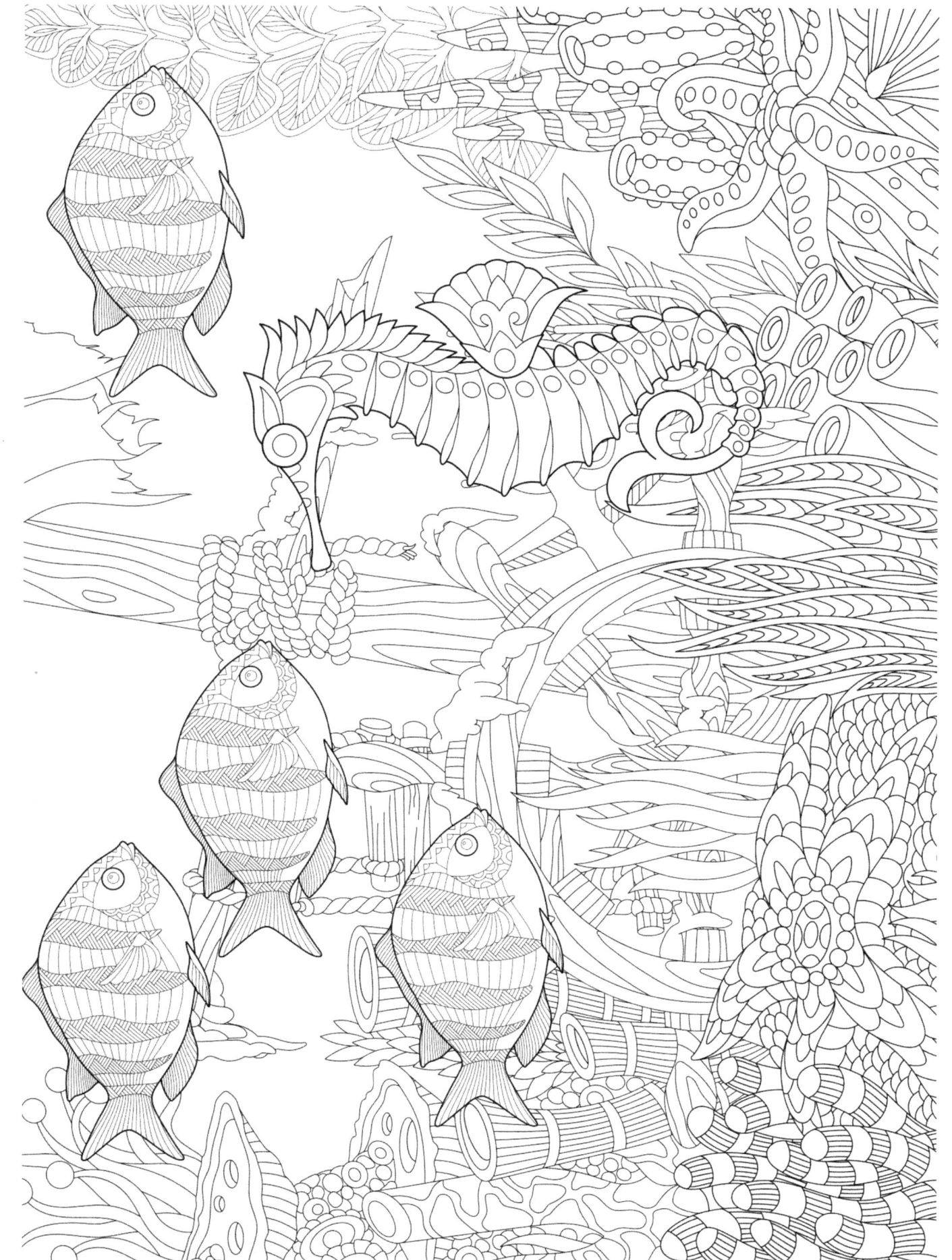

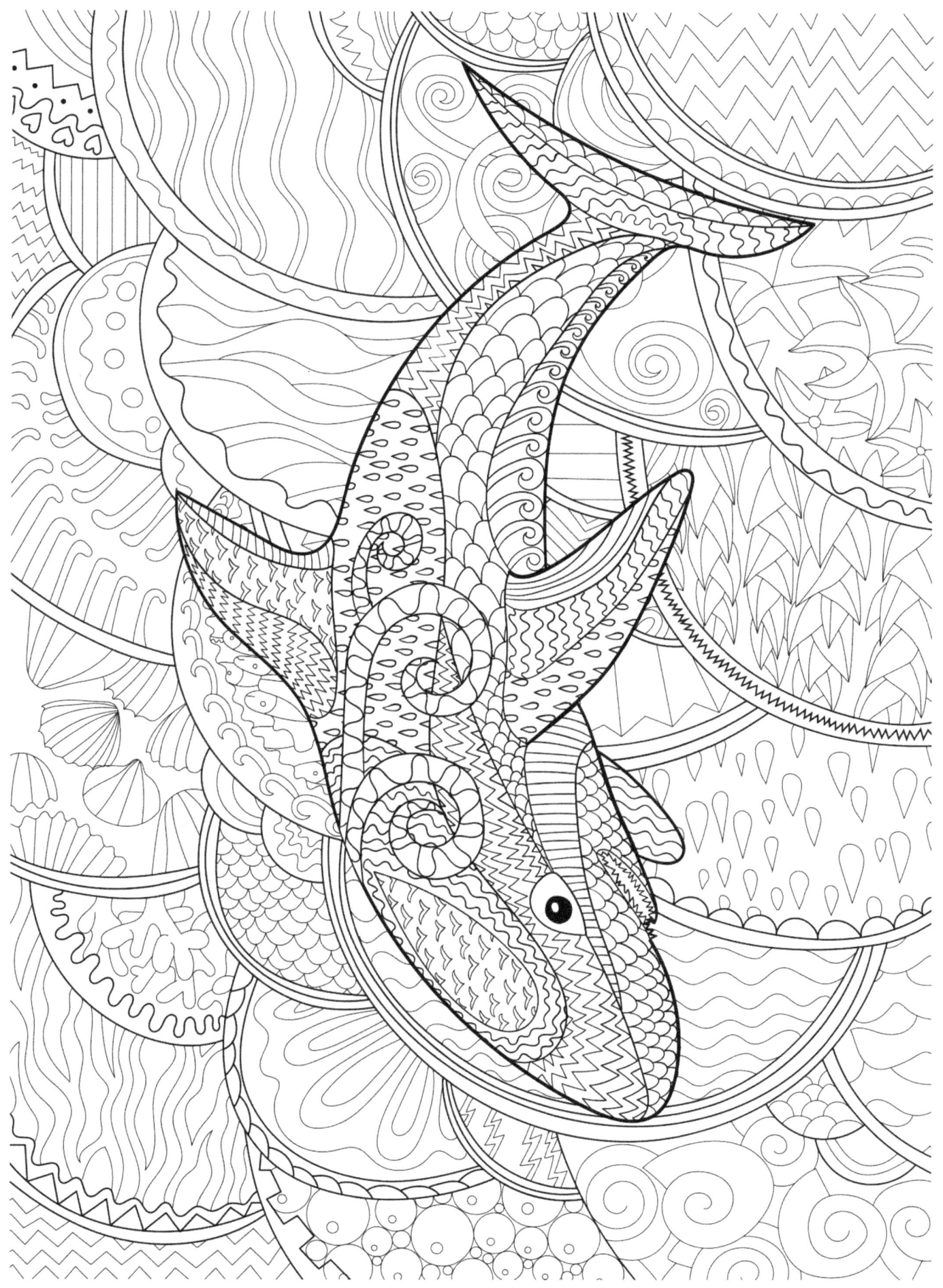

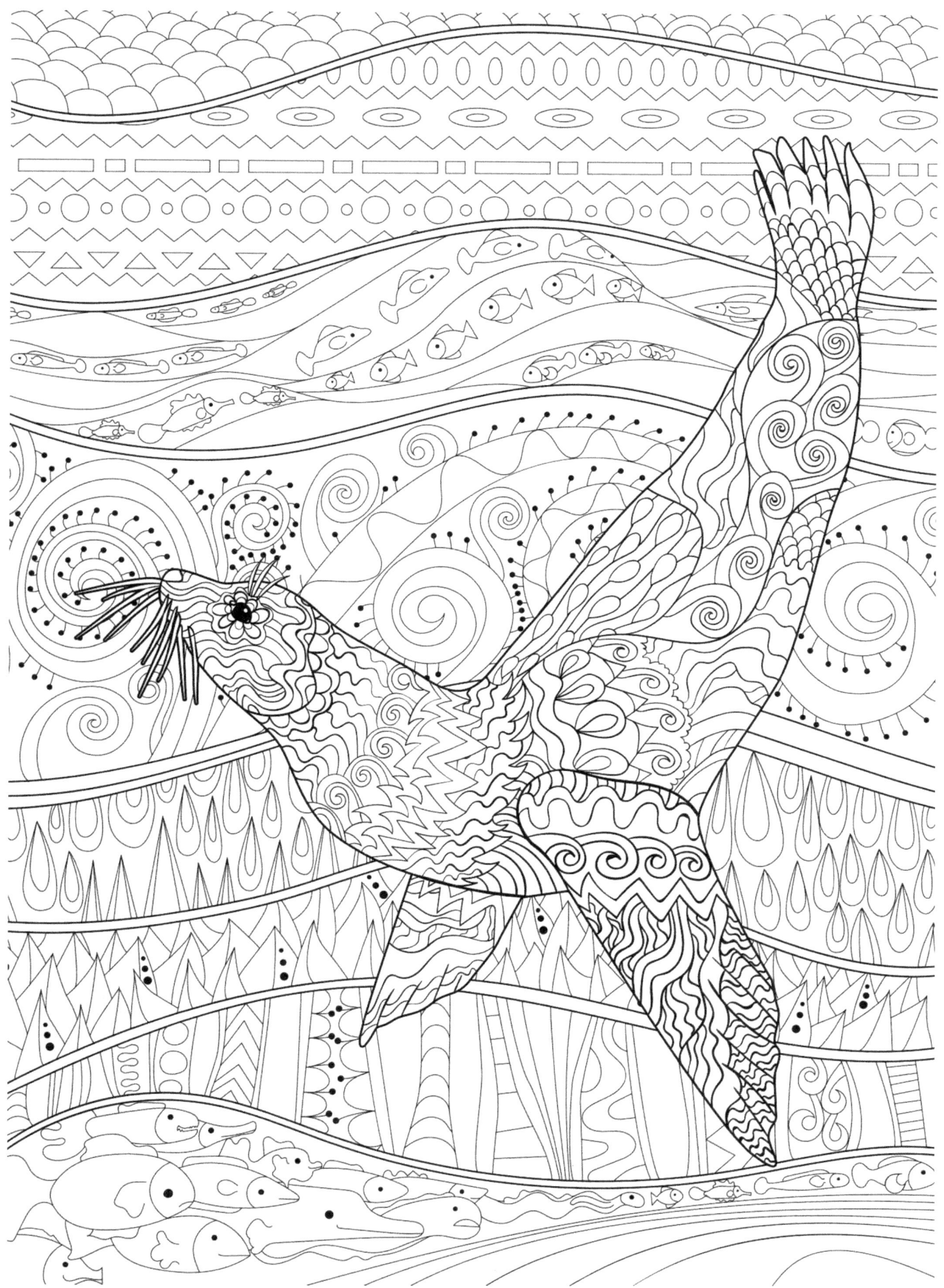

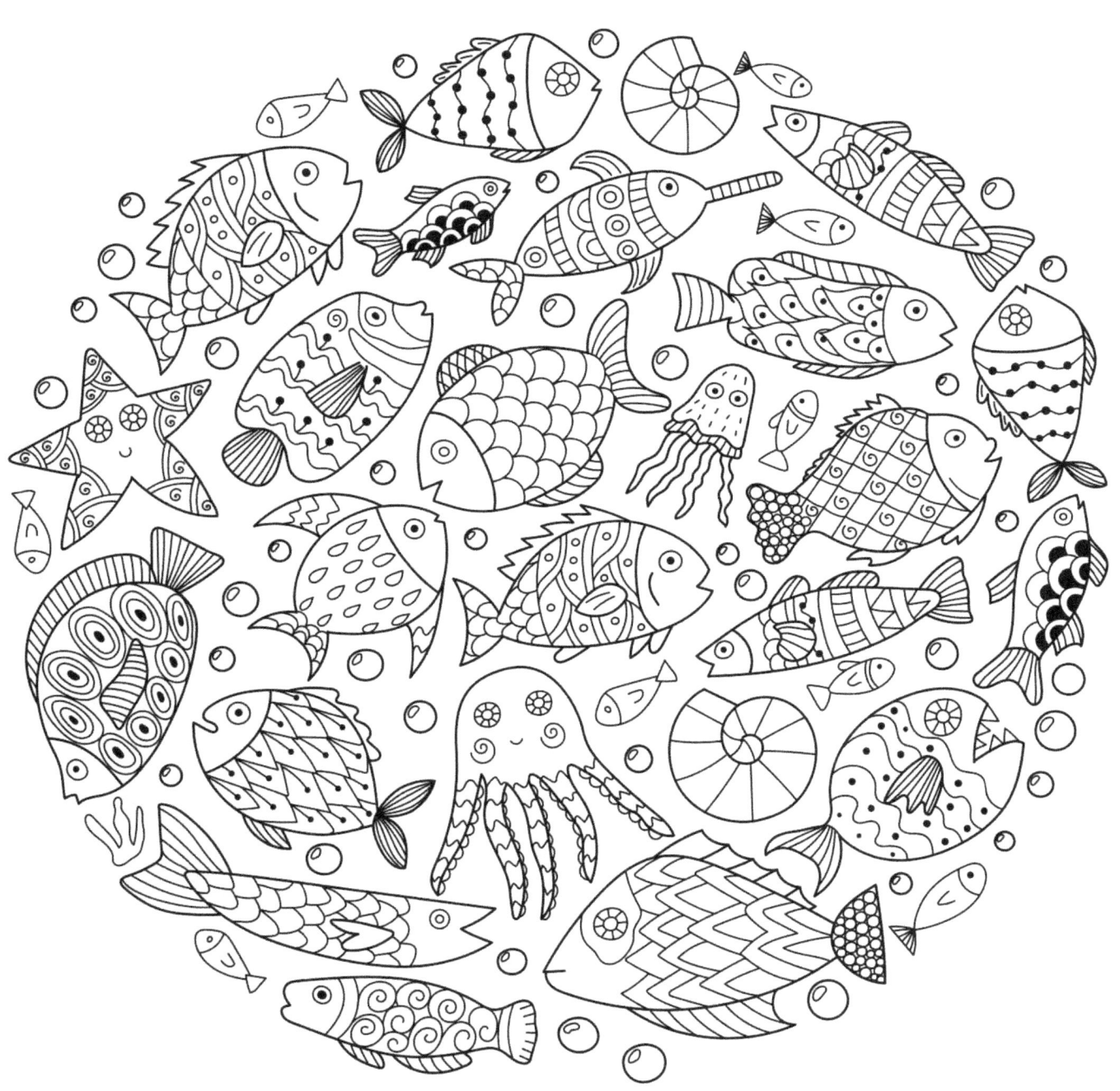

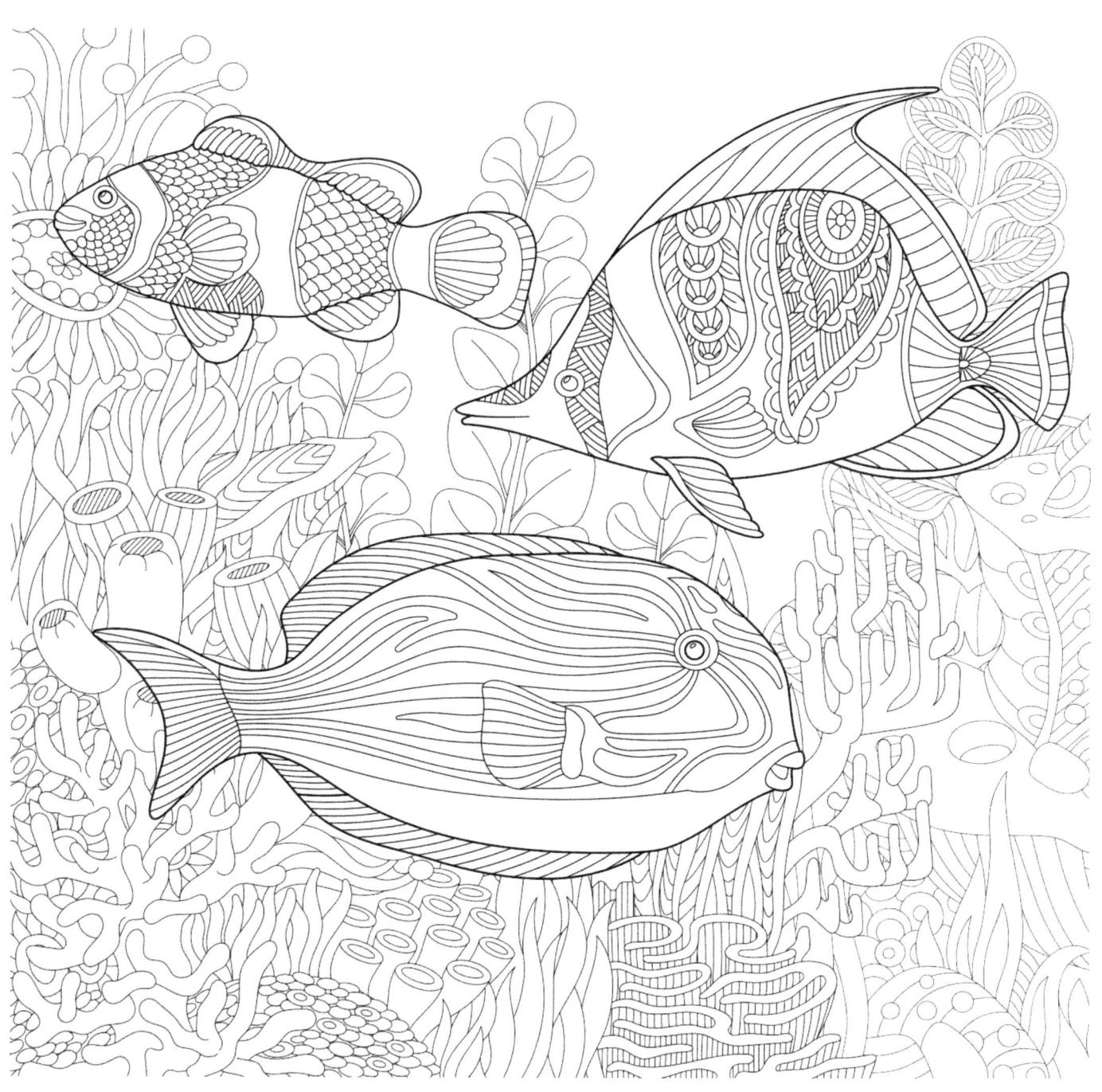

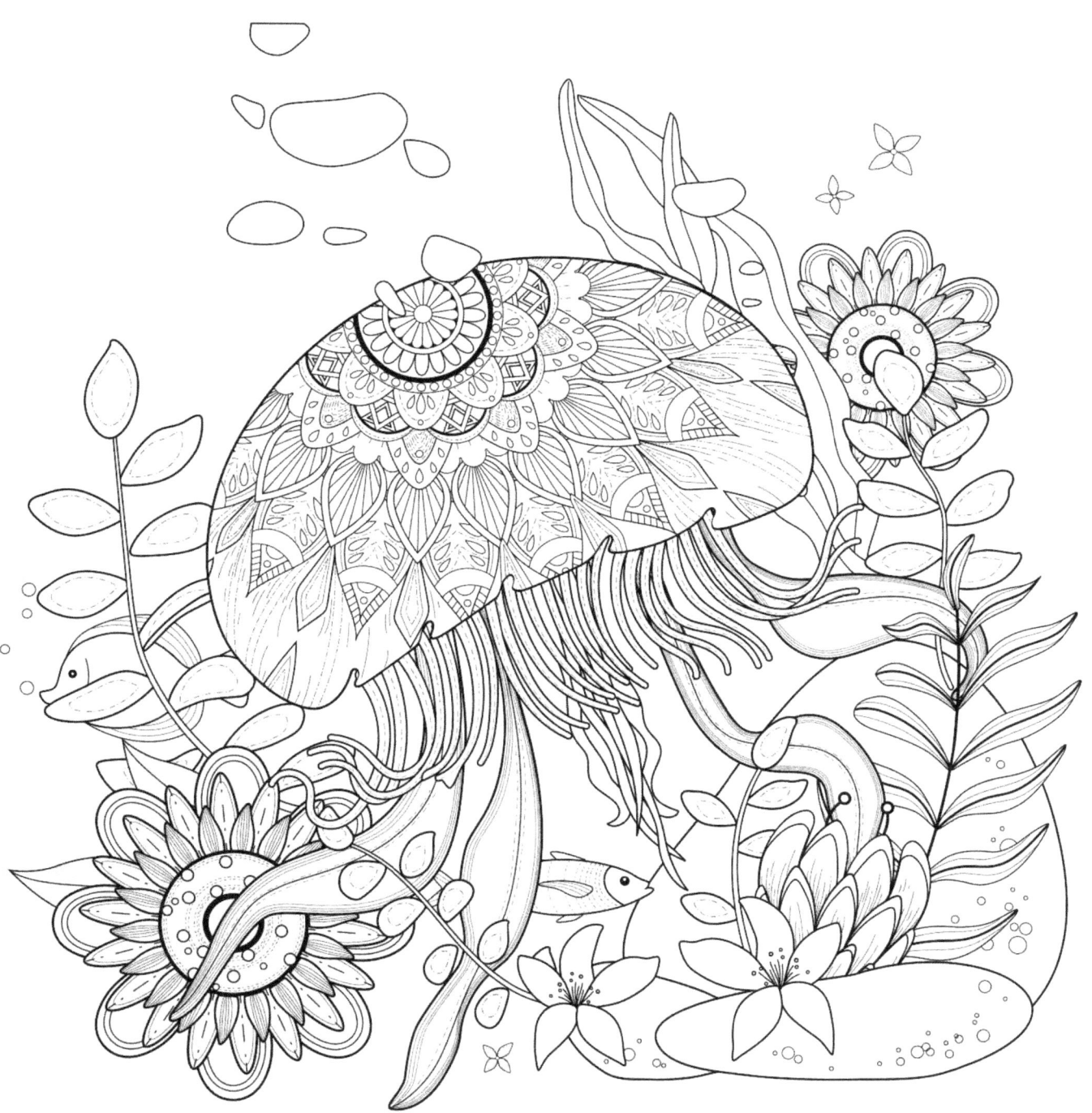

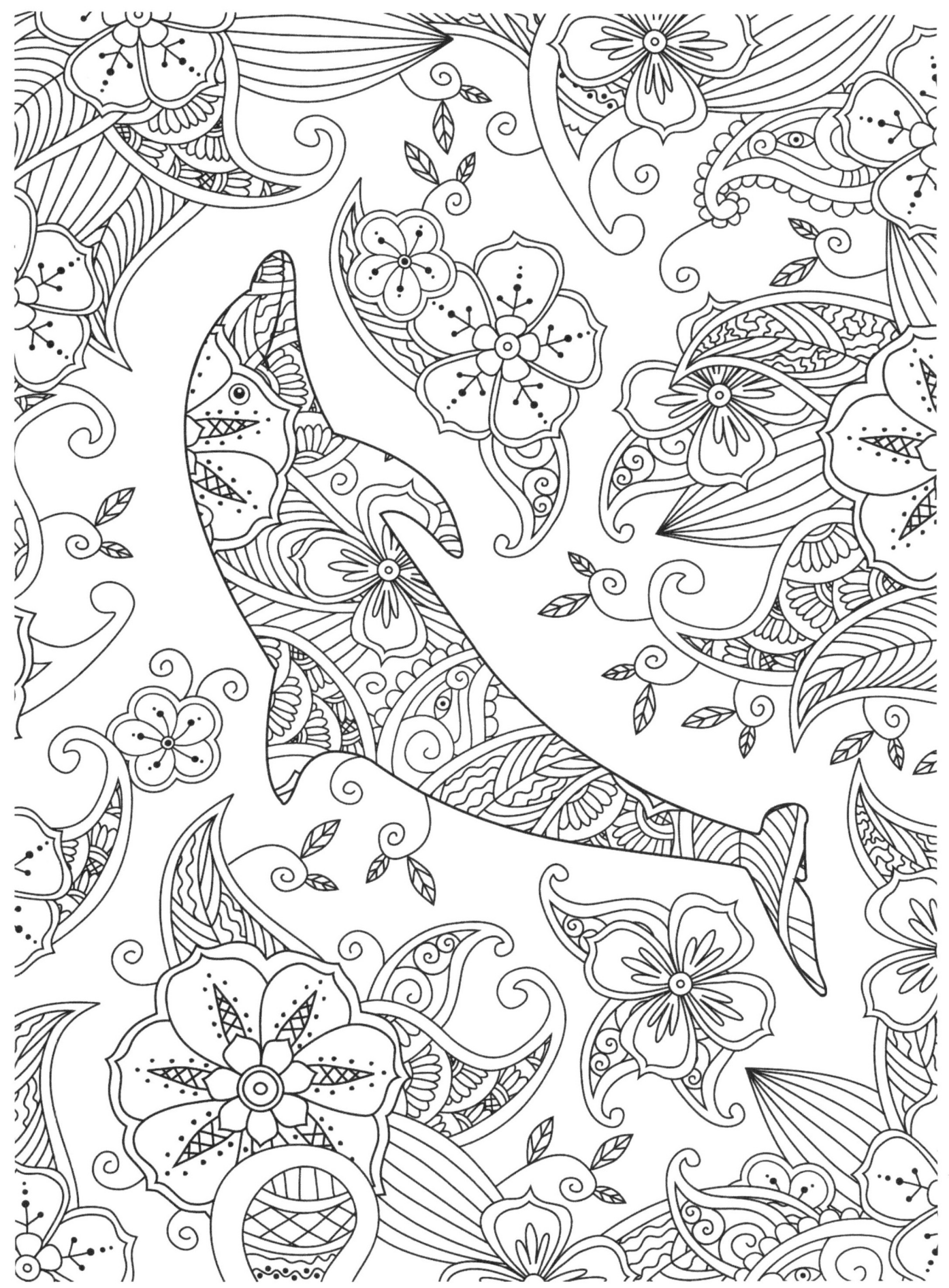

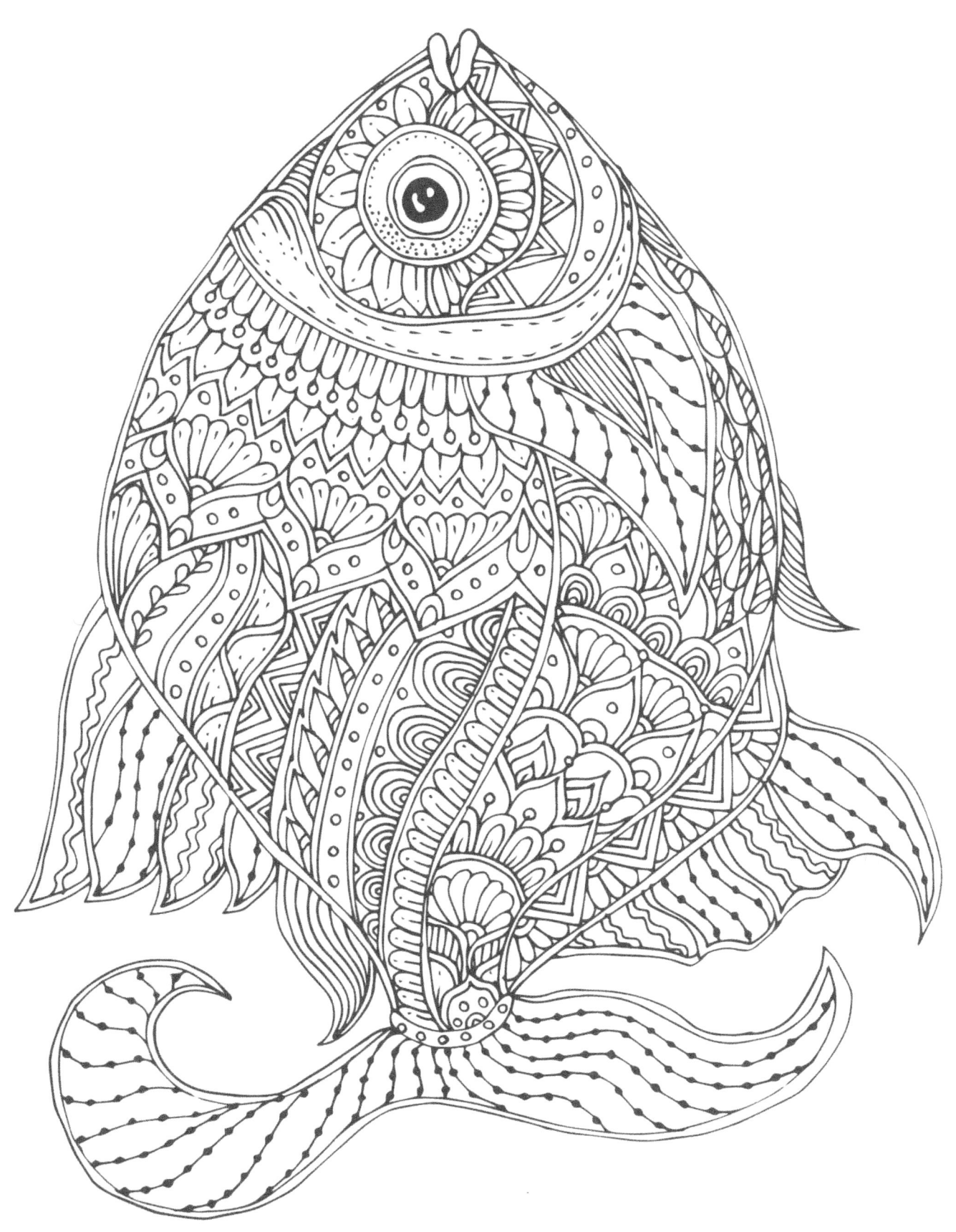

www.ingramcontent.com/pod-product-compliance
Lightning Source LLC
Chambersburg PA
CBHW081604280526
45788CB00011B/3554